NEW EMPLOYEE ORIENTATION

Charles M. Cadwell

CRISP PUBLICATIONS, INC.
Los Altos, California

NEW EMPLOYEE ORIENTATION

CREDITS
Editor: **Michael G. Crisp**
Designer: **Carol Harris**
Typesetting: **Interface Studio**
Cover Design: **Carol Harris**
Artwork: **Ralph Mapson**

Copyright © 1988 by Charles M. Cadwell
Printed in the United States of America

Crisp books are distributed in Canada by Reid Publishing, Ltd., P.O. Box 7267, Oakville, Ontario, Canada L6J 6L6.

In Australia by Career Builders, P.O. Box 1051 Springwood, Brisbane, Queensland, Australia 4127.

And in New Zealand by Career Builders, P.O. Box 571, Manurewa, New Zealand.

Library of Congress Catalog Card Number 87-73558
Cadwell, Charles M.
New Employee Orientation
ISBN 0-931961-46-7

PREFACE

This book will provide specific guidelines on how to conduct new employee orientation for any manager or supervisor. **New Employee Orientation** is not a guide about how to develop an employee handbook. There are several books available which can help you do that. Very few books, however, tell you how to conduct a logical, positive new employee orientation program. Too many organizations feel that giving a good company handbook to a new employee is a sufficient orientation. Although having an employee handbook is an *important* part of an effective orientation process, it is not a substitute for conducting a personal orientation.

Companies spend considerable money recruiting, interviewing, and often relocating new employees. Then, once a hiring decision has been made and the new employee arrives for work, most organizations provide very little formal attention to reinforce the employee's (often difficult) decision to accept the new position.

The guidelines provided in this book, if applied, will help a new employee feel welcome, learn the basics more quickly and become productive much sooner.

TO THE READER

NEW EMPLOYEE ORIENTATION is not like most books. It's not a book to read, it's a book to use. The unique ''self-paced'' format of this book and the many worksheets, encourage the reader to get involved and develop some new approaches to new employee orientation.

NEW EMPLOYEE ORIENTATION can be used effectively in a number of ways. Here are some possibilities:

—Self Study. Because the book is self-instructional, all that is needed is a quiet place, and some time. By completing the activities and exercises, a reader should not only receive valuable feedback, but also practical ideas about what to do when he/she has a new employee.

—Workshops and Seminars. The book is ideal for assigned reading prior to a workshop or seminar. With the basics in hand, the quality of the participation will improve, and more time can be spent on application during the program. The book is also effective when it is distributed at the beginning of a session, and participants ''work through'' the contents.

—Remote Location Training. Books can be sent to those not able to attend ''home office'' training sessions.

There are several other possibilities that depend on the objectives, program or ideas of the user.

One thing for sure, even after it has been read this book will be looked at—and thought about—again and again.

INTRODUCTION

One out of every five employees in the U.S. will quit his/her job this year. This translates to an average of 80,000 employees who have their first day on a new job, each work day of the year.

One reason people change jobs is that they never feel welcome or a part of the organization they join. As a result, many choose to switch, rather than fight, and simply quit their jobs and move on to another company shortly after they are hired. When this happens, the organization they leave behind is faced once again with the need to hire, orient and train another new employee. The cost of doing this has been estimated to be anywhere from $5,000 to $30,000 *per person*, depending upon the position in the organization.

A thoughtful new employee orientation program can reduce turnover and save an organization thousands of dollars. Whether a company has two employees or 20,000, it should not leave new employee orientation to chance.

More and more organizations are beginning to realize the positive benefits of utilizing part-time workers. Unfortunately they often think of these employees as not needing orientation, since they will only be there for a short while. This attitude often contributes to an even higher turnover rate.

New Employee Orientation outlines specific steps organizations can take to reduce both permanent and part-time employee turnover and at the same time quickly prepare workers for their new jobs. Reduced turnover along with better oriented and trained employees means better service for the customer. In today's service oriented economy a significant advantage can be provided to the company that uses the methods described in this book.

Just as you must develop a logical, thoughtful plan to start a successful business, you also need to take the same approach when orienting new employees.

If you apply the principles outlined in this book, you will learn how to:
—Evaluate your current orientation program;
—Begin your orientation during the interview process;
—Develop a plan for successful orientation;
—Orient both permanent and part-time employees.

Remember, when employees succeed, the organization succeeds. A thorough, well planned orientation is a first step on that road to success.

TABLE OF CONTENTS

PART I: THE BENEFITS OF PROPER ORIENTATION

OBJECTIVES

Objectives give us a sense of direction and purpose. They define what we want to accomplish and provide a way to measure our success. Objectives are a roadmap that takes us from where we are to where we want to be.

An effective new employee orientation program will accomplish the following objectives. It will:

☐ Provide a genuine welcome.

☐ Develop positive perceptions about the organization.

☐ Confirm the employee's decision to join the organization.

☐ Teach basic fundamentals each new employee should know.

☐ Provide a basis for training.

☐ Put the employee at ease.

In addition to these objectives, I want to:

_____

_____

_____

ARE YOU MEETING YOUR OBJECTIVES?

Think for a moment about the last few employees your organization hired, then honestly answer the questions below.

	Employee 1	Employee 2	Employee 3
Name:	_____	_____	_____
1. How long has each employee been on board?	_____	_____	_____
2. Do you think the employee was made to feel welcome?	Yes No	Yes No	Yes No
3. Do you think the employee regrets his/her decision to join your organization?	Yes No	Yes No	Yes No
4. Was the employee productive within a short period of time?	Yes No	Yes No	Yes No
5. Did your organization have a planned orientation program?	Yes No	Yes No	Yes No
6. If you had been in the employee's place, would you have been satisfied with the orientation?	Yes No	Yes No	Yes No

Circle the number that best describes the orientation these employees received.

1	2	3	4	5
POOR	NEEDS IMPROVEMENT	NOT SURE	GOOD	THE BEST

WHY A PLANNED ORIENTATION PAYS DIVIDENDS

Most new employees arrive for the first day of work full of enthusiasm and excitement. This initial interest can either be put to positive use, or destroyed, depending on how it is nurtured.

New employee orientation is not difficult and need not consume a large amount of time. In fact, when done properly, orientation will save time in the long run.

A poorly planned or non-existent orientation can quickly turn a carefully recruited and selected employee into another turnover statistic. If this occurs, it means more work for your organization because it will be necessary to start the entire employment process over.

A well planned and executed orientation on the other hand, will result in fewer mistakes and a better understanding of what is expected. This should lead to improved customer service, higher productivity and improved employee relations. Everyone wins— you, the employee, the organization, and most of all, your customers or clients.

The goal of orientation is to capitalize on each new employee's enthusiasm and keep it alive once the work begins. When orientation is successful, a new employee will become a valued asset to the organization.

WHY A PLANNED ORIENTATION PAYS DIVIDENDS (Continued)

Larger organizations are constantly hiring, orienting and training new employees. Many do it because they require seasonal help (i.e., Christmas, spring break, summer, etc.) during peak business periods. Others do it because of their reliance on inexperienced workers (i.e., fast food outlets, convenience stores, etc.). These workers change jobs frequently for a variety of reasons.

A well organized orientation can especially benefit organizations that need to orient large numbers of employees in short periods of time. Part IV of this book deals with specific things these organizations can do to develop a quality orientation program.

The balance of this first section will examine specific things any organization can do to meet the goals and objectives of new employee orientation.

To begin, it would be a good idea to review your own orientation. Often, we tend to imitate what we have experienced. If you received a good orientation, it is likely you will remember to pass along some of the items you experienced. If your orientation was poor, or lacking, this book can help you develop a positive program. Either way, by completing the exercises in the pages that follow, you will be better prepared to make new employees more productive and happier as they begin their careers.

(The facing page asks you to evaluate the orientation you received.)

HOW DID YOUR ORIENTATION RATE?

Think back to when you started your current job. Read each statement and circle either T (True) or F (False) as it relates to the orientation you received.

1. I was made to feel welcome.   T   F
2. I was introduced to other members of my work group.   T   F
3. My boss paid attention to me and made me feel welcome.   T   F
4. My orientation seemed well planned.   T   F
5. Company benefits were well explained the first day.   T   F
6. My office or work space was set up and waiting for me.   T   F
7. I received a tour of the organization by a qualified person.   T   F
8. All the necessary paperwork and forms were available, and I received
    assistance in completing them properly.   T   F
9. I received a copy of relevant literature, such as the company's
    Employee Handbook, Operations Manual, etc.   T   F
10. I learned about the company's history and future plans.   T   F
11. My boss reviewed my formal job description with me.   T   F
12. I was invited to lunch the first day by my boss or a key individual
    he/she selected.   T   F
13. I met people from other departments.   T   F
14. I was able to observe colleagues at work before starting a task.   T   F
15. I was given a specific job assignment along with instruction or training.   T   F
16. Office hours, dress code, sick leave and other policies were explained
    to me.   T   F
17. I was shown the phone system.   T   F
18. I had opportunities to ask questions.   T   F
19. Payroll policies (and withholding) were covered my first day.   T   F
20. At the end of the first week I felt like a member of the "team."   T   F

Total Number True: _____ False: _____

How did your orientation rate?

18-20 True: Your orientation was outstanding, I hope it was appreciated.

15-17 True: Your orientation was above average. You are in a position to make some improvements.

11-14 True: Unfortunately you received a typical orientation. There is a lot you can do to help your organization with future orientation.

10 or Less: You should be congratulated for sticking it out. Don't let the same thing happen to others.

PROVIDE A WELCOME

You never get a second chance to make a good first impression. Orientation is the time to roll out the red carpet. This simple act is often overlooked when a new employee arrives for work.

Why is it that most organizations hold elaborate "going away" parties when an employee leaves, (often to a competitor)? It suggests that leaving is a cause for celebration.

Wouldn't it be better to have a celebration when a new employee arrives? Why not have a party in the beginning to let the new employee get acquainted.

An easy way to provide such a welcome is to designate a room and time (usually an hour will be sufficient) to invite selected employees to meet the new person. Coffee and donuts add a nice touch.

This will make a new employee the center of attention at the beginning and provide an opportunity to meet key people in a relaxed, informal setting.

All members of the new employee's "team" should be encouraged to attend the gathering. They should be coached to go out of their way to make the new hire feel welcome. Nothing is worse than an insincere gathering where "veterans" talk with each other and exclude the newcomer. If this happens, it is better to postpone this event until everyone understands their roles.

Another way to make an employee feel welcome is to publicize the hiring decision. An announcement memo should be sent to all appropriate individuals or an article should be developed for the company newsletter. Information about the employee's background, family and specific job responsibilities is usually a good idea.

Most local newspapers have business sections that print information about promotions and new hires. Send or phone information to them when appropriate. For special hires, you might consider a press release with a photo to use with the story.

Making a new employee feel welcome is easy if you do some planning. The worksheet on the facing page will help you plan your welcome.

PLANNING WORKSHEET—
PROVIDING A WELCOME

List the items that need to be planned the next time you conduct a new employee orientation.

Welcoming Event: _____

_____

_____

Publicity: _____

_____

_____

Other Ideas: _____

_____

_____

Information checklist—Have you included?

____ Full name   ____ Previous work experience

____ Photo (if appropriate)   ____ Education (if appropriate)

____ Specific job title   ____ Effective start date

____ Immediate manager   ____ Spouse's name (if appropriate)

____ Special assignments   ____ Children and ages (if appropriate)

____ Other   ____ Hobbies, other interests

DEVELOP POSITIVE PERCEPTIONS

Orientation is a critical time. This is when a new employee develops perceptions about the organization, other employees, and you as a supervisor or manager.

It is critical to make a positive impression during this period. A planned and organized orientation will communicate that you are in control of the situation and the organization has definite quality standards.

New hires are naturally observant of the environment. They notice how well things are organized, whether a business-like atmosphere exists and whether it will be an enjoyable place to work. This initial opinion, once formed, can be hard to change. It is, therefore, essential that you do everything possible to create a positive perception.

When the new hire sees the real company, it should be the same one he/she saw during the recruiting and interviewing process. If this is not the case, the new employee will reconsider if this is the atmosphere in which he/she wants to work. Many new employees change their minds quickly without giving an organization the full benefit of their consideration because the job seems different from the one they expected. These expectations are usually based on perceptions generated during the interview.

Everything that happens the first few days will affect a new hire's perceptions and these will be passed on to friends, family and colleagues at the previous job. They will hear both the good and the bad. The quality of the orientation, therefore, is a reflection of an organization as much as any product or service that is offered.

Perceptions are especially important to part-time workers. These employees understand that if the job doesn't measure up they can move on to another organization.

You create positive perceptions by being organized and having a planned orientation.

WHAT PERCEPTION DO YOU CREATE?

Perceptions are made up of many factors. This questionnaire will help you evaluate the perceptions you create.

Circle Y (Yes) or N (No) depending on which best describes what a person would observe when visiting your work area.

1. Our work area is neat and organized.	Y	N
2. If a specific file is needed, it can be easily located.	Y	N
3. The whereabouts of all employees is known.	Y	N
4. When supervisors are out of the office, normal work continues.	Y	N
5. Employees are busy and appear to be doing productive work.	Y	N
6. Our employees are friendly and outgoing.	Y	N
7. Job applicants would receive an accurate picture of what our organization is like if they observed our work area for awhile.	Y	N
8. My family and friends think I work for a great organization.	Y	N
9. I say positive things about our operation to others.	Y	N
10. We can describe our new employee orientation program to job candidates.	Y	N

Total Number Yes: _____ No: _____

If you answered ''Yes'' to:

9 - 10: Excellent. You create a positive perception.

7 - 8: The perceptions you create are generally positive, but some improvement is possible.

5 - 6: You are sending out a negative message. Get to work.

4 or Less: Time to take a hard look at the perception you are creating. Things won't improve until you begin making some basic changes.

CASE STUDY

MARGE JACKSON
DEVELOPS NEW PERCEPTIONS

Marge Jackson waited in the reception area with great anticipation. She finally had been asked to interview for an administrative assistant position with Alpha-Omega Business Systems. She had heard it was a great place to work. She sent her resume in three months ago, but hadn't heard anything until two days ago. Although her interview with Sam Wilson wasn't scheduled to start until 11:30, she decided to get there 15 minutes early to make a good impression.

During her wait she observed several things about the company. The receptionist, Miss Parker, had greeted her warmly and offered her a cup of coffee. A few minutes later an employee, who was looking for a file, asked Miss Parker to help him. There was a discussion, some of it obviously toned down because of Marge's presence, which resulted in the employee storming out of the office. A few minutes later Miss Parker took a phone call and explained to the caller that Mr. Miller just left and she didn't know when he would return.

Just as she hung up another employee approached Miss Parker and the two began discussing last night's T.V. shows. When their discussion was finished, the employee came over to Marge and introduced herself as Jan Lock. She told Marge that she would really like working at Alpha-Omega, because the atmosphere was very relaxed and no one minded if you were a little bit late in the morning or left early in the afternoon.

At 11:45 Mr. Wilson appeared at Miss Parker's desk and asked if there were any messages for him. Miss Parker explained that Marge had been waiting to interview for the administrative assistant position since 11:30.

Mr. Wilson looked surprised. After a few seconds he walked over to Marge and explained that the position had been filled earlier that morning. He said he was sorry she had not been notified and hoped that she would keep Alpha-Omega in mind in the future.

CASE STUDY

(Continued)

What positive perceptions were created for Marge by Alpha-Omega?

_____

_____

_____

_____

What negative perceptions were created for Marge by Alpha-Omega?

_____

_____

_____

_____

How could Alpha-Omega improve the perceptions they create?

_____

_____

_____

_____

What type of orientation do you think Marge Jackson would have received if she had been hired by Alpha-Omega?

_____

_____

_____

_____

PART I: SELF ASSESSMENT

The following statements summarize key points presented in Part I. Check those that are true most of the time for you and your organization. Review all items not checked in order to improve future orientations.

_____ New employees remain enthusiastic after being on the job several months.

_____ New employee turnover is lower now than it was six months ago.

_____ I routinely take time to get to know my employees.

_____ Our company has an employee handbook which is kept up to date.

_____ All managers and supervisors have a plan for orienting new employees.

_____ Welcoming events are scheduled to help new employees get acquainted.

_____ Publicity about a new employee is routinely circulated.

_____ We create positive perceptions by keeping things organized.

_____ Our company has a reputation for being a great place to work.

_____ New employees have the opportunity to ask questions when they don't understand something.

Areas Where Improvement is Needed:

_____

_____

_____

You can probably think of situations in which what you expected and what actually happened were totally different. You may have left (or at least considered leaving) a job because of the poor orientation you received.

New employee orientation must be planned. New employees are willing and eager to learn. If you don't have a plan to use their enthusiasm you can quickly dampen their spirits. Don't let that happen. Get them started right and you'll increase the chance of developing a positive, long-term working relationship.

PART II: | PLANNING FOR SUCCESS

PLANNING FOR SUCCESS

When you plan for success, you are more likely to achieve it. This section of the book will discuss the factors you can use to your advantage when planning a new employee orientation program.

Confirm Job Decision

Orientation is a great way to allow the new employee to confirm that he/she has made the right employment choice. An employee will be looking for assurance from you to reinforce the decision of choosing your company as the place to work.

In all likelihood your new employee interviewed with other organizations. Since you felt the person was a good choice, others may have also. The decision to select your organization may have been a difficult one, so the first day is a perfect time to reinforce the employee's decision to work for you.

How many times have you seen (or heard about) a new employee leaving a new job within a few weeks? It is not uncommon. Usually the reason given is, ''This wasn't what I expected.'' Most turnover of this type occurs during the first month. This is especially true of businesses that hire hourly workers. Part IV discusses the special problems of orientation in high turnover environments. If the employee survives the first month, the chances of a long-term relationship are improved. You will significantly increase the chances of keeping a new employee when an orientation plan clearly spells out your expectations.

The initial expectations that are communicated have a decided impact on an employee's job performance. If you expect quality performance and communicate it by both word and deed, you increase the probability of getting high performance. On the other hand, if you communicate low expectations, that's what you're likely to receive.

You control a new employee's expectations. If you developed expectations during the recruiting process that are not realistic, you will soon find yourself with the same job opening. Keep in mind that every interaction you have with a potential employee communicates expectations and sets an example.

WERE YOUR EXPECTATIONS MET?

Think back to when you started your current job. How well did your company meet your expectations for each item listed?

5—Exceeded expectations

4—Met expectations

3—Partially met expectations

2—Left a lot to be desired

1—Missed completely

_____ 1. Introductions to others

_____ 2. Tour of work place

_____ 3. Friendliness of co-workers

_____ 4. Helpfulness of supervisor/manager

_____ 5. Organized work area

_____ 6. First job assignment

_____ 7. Explanation of how things work

_____ 8. Help in relocating (if applicable)

_____ 9. Explanation of benefits

_____ 10. Planned orientation

Note any item that you rated as 3 or less. These are areas you need to plan in advance in order to meet the expectations of your new employees. For those items you rated as 4 or 5, be sure to continue the positive approach that you received.

DEFINE YOUR EXPECTATIONS

One orientation goal is to help the employee confirm that he/she made the right decision to work for you.

On the previous page you evaluated how well your expectations were met. How about your expectations for those you hire? Answer the questions below to help clarify your expectations for a new employee.

What specific job expectations do you have for new employees?

_____

_____

_____

How do you communicate these expectations in a positive manner during the recruiting process?

_____

_____

_____

How do you communicate your expectations the first day?

_____

_____

_____

How do you communicate your expectations the first week?

_____

_____

_____

SET THE STAGE FOR TRAINING

Orientation is the time to get the employee started on the right foot. A well planned program will set the stage for all training that follows. A thoughtful orientation should answer most basic questions a new employee might have. When this happens, attention can be focused on teaching skills needed to perform a job.

Without a well planned orientation program, new employees are forced to learn on their own. This can be time consuming and inefficient. Often an employee will lack some essential information or receive incorrect or misleading information. If an orientation program is lacking or poorly planned, considerable time will be wasted re-inventing the wheel.

When given proper direction, a clear assignment, and specific information, a new employee is more likely to get started correctly and will be more receptive when it is time to begin training.

Orientation should provide a new employee with the necessary information about his/her role in the organization. This is best done in a one-on-one meeting but can be accomplished in a group session.

PUTTING THE EMPLOYEE AT EASE ON THE FIRST DAY

The first day on the job is filled with anxiety and uncertainty for most new employees. Almost all want to make a good first impression and do things right. In an effort to fit in, some new employees may say or do things that seem forced or brash. Others will react just the opposite. They may fear doing or saying the wrong thing and consequently won't do anything without being specifically asked or directed.

One of the best ways to keep things relaxed is to introduce everyone in a friendly, relaxed environment. The sooner a new employee gets to know his/her co-workers, the better. The earlier people know each other the better the chances of a positive long-term working relationship.

It is important to verbalize that the organization is pleased the new employee is on board. If the employee feels confident that he/she will fit in and be able to make important contributions a positive perception has been created.

It is also a good idea to reinforce that help is available if there are any questions. Take time to answer questions and provide clear direction. Do everything in your power to help the new employee succeed.

TAKE TIME TO ANSWER QUESTIONS
AND PROVIDE CLEAR DIRECTION

PLANNING THE ORIENTATION

In the space provided, indicate how you plan to accomplish each of the following objectives during the orientation you conduct.

_____ Provide Clear Direction About Job Expectations

_____

_____

_____

_____

_____ Explain Organization Structure

_____

_____

_____

_____

_____ Make First Job Assignment

_____

_____

_____

_____

_____ Give Specific Background Information

_____

_____

_____

_____

CASE STUDY

SUSAN BEAL'S EXPECTATIONS

Susan Beal, the new accounting supervisor, arrived for her first day of work at Accounting Unlimited with expectations for a great first day. As she drove to work she envisioned a day full of learning about the company, its plans for the future and the role she would play in helping the company succeed. She couldn't wait to get started.

Susan's boss, Joan Parker, met her at 8:00 a.m. and brought Susan a cup of coffee. Joan suggested they start the day with a tour of the office. Just as they were starting, Joan's secretary came in with an urgent message. Joan's boss needed to see her right away to discuss the revised budget. Joan took Susan to meet Mark Langston, another account supervisor and one of Susan's co-workers. She asked Mark to take Susan on the tour and said she would be back shortly to continue the orientation.

Mark was very busy and appeared annoyed at being interrupted. He agreed, however, to take Susan on the office tour while Joan went to the meeting with her boss. Mark's tour lasted just 5 minutes and included several comments about how hard it was to to get things done with all the interruptions.

Mark took Susan to her new office area and told her to wait there for Joan to return. Susan waited and waited. Finally at 10:30 Joan returned and told Susan there were problems and her meeting would last until at least noon. She handed Susan several project files and suggested Susan read through them until she returned. If Susan had any questions she was to talk to Mark.

CASE STUDY

(Continued)

Consider Susan Beal's situation and answer these questions:

What was positive about Susan's orientation?

_____

_____

_____

What impression do you think Susan has of Accounting Unlimited?

_____

_____

_____

What impression do you think Susan has of her new boss?

_____

_____

_____

How could the situation have been avoided?

_____

_____

_____

How can Joan Parker recover from the problems of the morning?

_____

_____

_____

SUMMARY

An effective orientation should take advantage of a new employee's enthusiasm and keep it alive. As the supervisor, you have the most immediate impact on creating a positive environment. You accomplish this by developing a well planned orientation.

An effective orientation should meet these objectives:

☐ Provide a genuine welcome.

☐ Develop positive perceptions about the organization.

☐ Confirm the employee's decision to join the organization.

☐ Teach basic fundamentals each new employee should know.

☐ Provide a basis for training.

☐ Put the employee at ease.

These objectives can be achieved by using the procedures outlined in the next section. Before proceeding, however, take a few minutes to answer the situation presented on the next two pages. If you can answer these questions you are on your way to conducting an effective new employee orientation.

REVIEW

The next time I conduct a new employee orientation, I will plan ahead as follows:

I will provide a welcome by:

_____

_____

_____

_____

SUMMARY (Continued)

I can develop positive perceptions by:

_____

_____

_____

_____

I will establish positive, realistic expectations by:

_____

_____

_____

_____

I plan to reinforce the job decision by:

_____

_____

_____

_____

I will lay the foundation for subsequent training by:

_____

_____

_____

_____

I will put the employee at ease by:

_____

_____

_____

_____

PART III: ORIENTATION FOR PERMANENT EMPLOYEES

DO IT RIGHT AND ONLY DO IT ONCE

Someone in your organization (maybe you), spent considerable time reviewing resumes and applications. Additional time was spent interviewing for an open decision. Then a decision had to be made about the right person for the job.

Now the person that was selected for your job is ready to go to work and it is time for an orientation program. This section will help you establish or refine such a program.

A successful orientation process should be customized to fit the particular needs of an organization and a new employee. Successful programs are carefully planned and implemented so they are done once and done right. Otherwise a poor impression is the result and productivity will suffer.

Start Orientation During the Interview

The interview process is where orientation begins. When a job is discussed with the applicant, the following items, at a minimum, should be covered:

—Background of the Organization,

—General Job Description,

—Performance Evaluation Procedures,

—Work Hours,

—Compensation,

—Vacation and Time Off,

—Benefits,

—Probation Period.

DO IT RIGHT AND ONLY DO IT ONCE
(Continued)

Each of these items plus any others you feel are pertinent should be discussed and available in written form if the prospective employee wishes. These represent basic considerations that any applicant wants to know before making an informed decision about joining a company. By covering these points before a job offer is made, you provide a chance for the prospective hire to evaluate the job objectively.

Often an applicant may decide the job is not suitable based on the factors presented during the interview. If an applicant withdraws from consideration because of a disagreement about the job basics, you have probably come out ahead. This is far better than investing orientation and training time, only to lose the new employee the first month because he/she had a problem with the terms and conditions of employment.

Start your orientation during the interview process and you will save time and energy that can be devoted to employees who know what the job offers.

Consider a Prospective Employee Kit

You can save valuable time by preparing a friendly package of documents for prospective employees. This "kit" can be given during the interview process to help an applicant decide if he/she would be a good fit with the company.

Such a kit can be used throughout your organization by anyone who has contact with prospective employees.

If you already have a set of handouts for prospective employees, use the checklist on the following page to ensure it is complete.

DOES YOUR PROSPECTIVE EMPLOYEE KIT INCLUDE?

Name, address and phone number of organization	Yes	No
Names and titles of key executives	Yes	No
A brief history of the organization	Yes	No
Normal working hours	Yes	No
Pay periods	Yes	No
Vacation and time off policies	Yes	No
Medical and other benefits	Yes	No
Type of new hire probation period	Yes	No
Contact person following the interview	Yes	No
Specific job description*	Yes	No
Specific salary information*	Yes	No

For out of town interviewees, do you have?

General information about the neighborhood or city	Yes	No
Address and phone number of Chamber of Commerce	Yes	No
Names and numbers of several reputable realtors	Yes	No
Name of placement bureaus (for spouse)	Yes	No

*Provided separate from the standard kit.

ORIENTATION TEMPLATE

On page 74 of this book is an ''Orientation Template.'' It is provided for you to use while developing a complete orientation plan. There are also several checklists to help you develop a customized plan for your organization.

Each new employee is different. Each has a specific set of skills and aptitudes. Each has a unique personality. Your orientation will be more effective if you take individual differences into account. However, in addition to being sensitive to individual differences, you must also develop a standardized list of items. Your challenge therefore, is to address an individual's needs, yet use a standardized approach to insure all bases are covered. There are several ways to accomplish this goal.

The best orientation is one that involves the employee to the fullest extent possible. If you give a new employee the opportunity to feedback what he/she most wants to learn, the prospects for an excellent orientation are significantly increased.

One way to accomplish this is by asking the applicant several questions during the interview. For example, you might ask, ''What would you like to learn first?'' ''What are your expectations for the first day?'' ''What projects are you most interested in learning about?''

INVOLVE THE EMPLOYEE

Involving the new employee can also be done at the beginning of the orientation by presenting a schedule of items you intend to cover and asking which are most relevant. This way the new employee knows what is planned and has an opportunity to add other items or issues. He or she will also see that you have taken time to make the orientation meaningful.

Another consideration is to schedule aspects of the program around the employee's work schedule. The person making the job assignments should stagger the orientation so it will not conflict with an employee's new responsibilities. Essential information, plus that which the employee is most interested in, can be covered early and the employee will be able to cover the rest over time.

The checklists and template on pages 72 and 74 are excellent starting points. Each item on the list should determine what specific information you need to properly cover that topic with a new employee. Remember, your job is to personalize the orientation process to meet the specific needs of each employee.

ORIENTATION IS AN ON-GOING PROCESS

Orientation is not a one day event. It normally is a process that continues for several days or weeks.

Think how long it took for you to become comfortable in your job. Chances are it took several weeks to feel in command of your job responsibilities and even longer to understand how your new company operated. You learned new things continually. It is therefore, not realistic to expect a new employee to be oriented in just a few days, no matter how well you put your plan together.

As previously noted, the first day is critical. Getting the process started on the right foot will ensure the day will be remembered positively. First days are *always* remembered.

If you ask colleagues about their first day, often what you hear will be negative, such as not knowing where to park, which door to enter, finding your boss out of town that day or just being given a bunch of forms to fill out. All of these situations can be avoided with planning.

CASE STUDY

CASE STUDY

MARY'S ORIENTATION

Mary showed up for work bright and early her first day. After a few introductions, she was told by her new boss to go to a nearby office supply store and buy herself a desk and some supplies. She was instructed to have it delivered by two o'clock.

Mary's boss gave her the name of the office supply store, but no information on what to buy or how much to spend.

She found the store, selected and purchased a desk that was delivered at exactly two o'clock. Somehow the cost of the desk was within the unknown budget.

Mary's first official act was a success, and she subsequently became a valued employee. Many new employees faced with a similar assignment would not be as resourceful as Mary because of the ambiguity. Mary's boss was lucky because Mary could have spent a small fortune or else walked away from a company that was so loosely run.

If you were Mary—what would your reaction have been?

THE FIRST DAY ON THE JOB

As you plan your orientation program, strive to make the first day memorable in a positive way. Get things started correctly. When this happens, the rest of the orientation will be more effective and go smoother.

One mistake to avoid is trying to cram everything the new employee needs to know into the first day. Schedule the orientation over several days. Give each employee enough time to assimilate new information in a way that is meaningful.

New employees are nervous the first day. This may make it difficult for them to remember everything if you try to cover too much information too soon.

One suggestion is to provide written information, such as an employee handbook containing basic information that can be referred to later. Take time to go over critical items in any written information and encourage questions.

Watch for pitfalls as you plan

YOUR FIRST DAY ON THE JOB

Your experience can be an excellent source of ideas on what to do and what *not* to do the first day. Think back to the orientation you received the first day in your present job and list the good and not so good things you remember.

Good	Not So Good
_____	_____
_____	_____
_____	_____
_____	_____
_____	_____

For each item in the "Not So Good" column, describe below how you plan to ensure your new employee receives a good experience in that area. Be sure to remember all the "Good" things you experienced and repeat them.

1. _____

_____

2. _____

_____

3. _____

_____

4. _____

_____

5. _____

_____

HOW TO HAVE A SUCCESSFUL NEW EMPLOYEE ORIENTATION

Your Role as a Supervisor

Once a job has been accepted and a starting date has been agreed upon, the first thing to do is clear your schedule. Orientation is not a time to be out of town or locked up in meetings.

As a supervisor, you are responsible for getting things started during orientation. It is not the responsibility of a secretary or another employee to do your job. They may be involved, but the new employee should not be assigned to anyone until you have made the initial contact and established a plan for the day.

Make Time to Meet

A breakfast meeting is a unique way to welcome the employee. Properly planned, breakfast will allow you to meet in a relaxed setting where you can provide an overview of what the day will hold.

Be on time. If you are late for your first meeting, you will communicate that being on time is not important. Do everything you can to put the employee at ease.

You set the example for everything that happens the first day. What you do or don't do, what you say or don't say, will be noticed and remembered. The standards you demonstrate will be quickly communicated by your actions.

Your role during orientation must be an active one. Devote as much time as possible on the first day to the new employee.

Avoid Interruptions

Your initial meeting should be arranged in a place and at a time that avoids interruptions. This will allow you to devote full attention to the employee.

We are all individuals and want to be treated as such. New employees should be made to feel as if they are the most important people you have to see. They should never feel like an interruption to busy schedules. As you meet with each new hire, avoid looking at your watch or talking about all you have to do.

Allow enough time so you won't have to hurry through things. Spending quality time with the new employee will pay dividends in the future.

HOW TO HAVE A SUCCESSFUL NEW EMPLOYEE ORIENTATION (Continued)

Staff Orientation

Orientation will include the other parts of an organization. A new employee needs a good overview of how things work and where basic responsibilities lay. A good way to do this is with an overview session which includes representatives from key departments.

This will give new employees the opportunity to meet people outside of their immediate work group. It also provides different perspectives about the organization's products, services, and/or goals. The objective is for each new employee to develop an appreciation about how the organization functions.

To make such meetings productive, new employees should be encouraged to develop a list of questions to ask each group that is represented. You may wish to provide a list of suggested questions to ensure each employee's orientation time is focused. A prepared list of questions will make it easier for new employees to participate in the meetings.

Some sample questions include:
—What is the responsibility of your department?
—To whom do you report?
—Who reports to you?
—With which departments do you most frequently interact?
—What major projects are currently involving you?
—What are barriers you face in getting your job done?
—What type of interaction do you have with my new department?
—Will we be meeting again?

The best time to schedule staff overview meetings is after an employee has worked a few days. By then that person will know more about the company and be in a better position to ask pertinent questions.

Consider asking a key executive (such as the president) to provide the final overview of the organization's goals and an informal ''state of the state'' report. This can be a great way to provide a real feeling of importance for new employees.

COMPANY HISTORY

Normally it is a good idea to provide more background on how the company got started, significant events in the company's development (i.e. when an important product was launched; how the organization decided to diversify, etc.). Company history, traditions, and culture should be presented in a positive manner.

The goal is to give new employees a sense of identity with the organization. How did it get to where it is today? Who were the founders? What has the growth been like? What is the mission of the organization? Each new employee should have a sense of how the past paved the way for what is happening today.

New employees should feel a sense of pride about past accomplishments. Well presented, a company history will reinforce the decision that joining your company was the best possible choice.

Some large organizations have slide shows or videos available to present the company's story. Be sure any session emphasizes how new employees fit into the future plans of the company. Let each employee feel like part of the future growth.

THE ORGANIZATION'S HISTORY

The history of an organization should provide a new employee with a sense of pride in being selected to join the team. The message should be positive and upbeat. The following worksheet can help you prepare your organization's story.

Parent Company (if applicable) _____

_____

Official Company Name _____

What the Name Represents _____

Organizational Mission _____

_____

Company Philosophy _____

_____

Notable Achievements _____

_____

Date Founded _____

Founders _____

Company Size Originally _____

Company Size Now _____

Original Products/Services _____

_____

Current Products/Services _____

_____

Recent Accomplishments _____

_____

Goals For the Future _____

_____

TOUR THE WORKPLACE

Shortly after starting work the new employee should be given a tour of the workplace. During the interview the job candidate may have received a glimpse of the work area. Now is the time to provide an insider's view. Your objective during the tour is to develop a feeling of being a part of a team.

During the tour, be sure to spend time where other members of the new employee's team are located. Take time to introduce the new employee to each person. Some friendly ''personalizing'' comments (i.e. ''Sandy is our company softball captain.'') help break the ice.

It is a good idea to let others know approximately what time you will be starting your tour. This way they can make it a point to be available for an introduction.

The tour should include the entire facility. Briefly visit each major area and explain how to gain access to the area when necessary. Companies with large facilities sometimes prepare a map for new employees that specifies the correct parking lot, entrance, etc..

Don't overlook any area that relates to the new employee's job. Remember, the sooner the new employee knows where things are and how they work, the sooner that person will be productive.

Many new employees unnecessarily have to ask people they don't know where to find the bathroom, a copy machine, or the lunch room. Use a Tour Guide Worksheet similar to the one on the next page to make sure you properly plan your tour of the workplace.

TOUR GUIDE WORKSHEET

Check off each item you need to include on your tour of the work place. Add any others not on the list.

_____ Office area	_____ Conference area
_____ Co-workers	_____ Cafeteria
_____ Secretary	_____ Executive offices
_____ Map of facility	_____ Restricted areas
_____ Stairs	_____ Copy machine
_____ Elevators	_____ Supply area
_____ Fire exits	_____ Receptionist
_____ Storm shelter	_____ Word processing center
_____ Mailroom	_____ Files
_____ Vending	_____ Break area
_____ Restrooms	_____ Storage
_____ Parking lots	_____ Conference room
_____ _____	_____ _____
_____ _____	_____ _____
_____ _____	_____ _____
_____ _____	_____ _____

COMPLETE PAPERWORK

Sometime the first day it is important to have the new employee complete the necessary paperwork for payroll, health benefits, and other items. This is the time to make sure all loose ends are completed. If an employee application is not on file, get one processed. If the employee needs an I.D. card or a key to gain access to the building, have one available.

Although these paperwork items may seem trivial, they can cause real problems later if not taken care of now. Otherwise it may be necessary to explain why the employee's first check is late or why a family member's visit to the doctor wasn't covered by insurance.

If there are some paperwork items that can be completed later, they can be given to the employee along with specific deadlines for completion. Items such as association memberships or the circulation list for periodicals can wait until the employee gets settled in the job.

JOB DESCRIPTION/ORGANIZATION CHART

Also during the first day, arrange a meeting where the new employee receives a copy of his/her job description. Take time to answer any questions the employee has.

Carefully review the purpose of the job description, namely:

—Describes what is expected of you by the company;

—Clearly defines responsibilities;

—Helps focus on priorities;

—Helps define what training is needed to do the job;

—Provides a way by which to evaluate job performance.

Be sure the employee understands clearly the specific duties and responsibilities of the job and what is expected.

A complete job description will describe how the employee's duties contribute to the success of the department and the company.

A copy of the company and department organization chart should also be provided which explains how the new employee's work group fits into the total organization structure. This chart should clearly define responsibilities and assignments so employees can see at a glance where their job fits and what the working relationships are among the various departments.

ASSIGN A TASK

Many supervisors make the mistake of not involving a new employee with some actual work the first day. Often, instead of being given meaningful work, new employees are handed stacks of papers and manuals to read which will ''acquaint'' them with the job. More likely the result will be boredom. Instead of being challenged an employee can quickly become disillusioned if given nothing but busy work.

New employees are eager to demonstrate their skills. Wise managers take advantage of this situation and get the employee actively involved in current projects as soon as possible.

An early assignment that provides a sense of achievement is a great idea, especially if it is followed up later with words of encouragement. Make it a point to acknowledge what the employee has done. Pay attention to the results and comment on them. This increases the likelihood that the employee will continue to work at the same high level in the future.

Since a new employee wants to make a good first impression, make every effort to provide the opportunity to allow the new employee to show his/her stuff.

TAKE TO LUNCH

If your orientation was designed to cover the objectives outlined in this section, a new employee may feel overwhelmed by lunch time. He/she will be ready for a break and an opportunity to reflect on what has been covered. It is an excellent time to provide answers to any questions resulting from the activities of the morning.

Make every attempt the first day not to leave the new employee alone at lunch time. If you cannot be present, then make sure someone has been assigned to take the employee to lunch. It's a nice gesture if the company buys lunch the first day.

If you weren't able to meet the employee for breakfast, lunch is a good second choice. You may consider inviting selected co-workers to help establish the feeling of teamwork. Lunch should be as positive and relaxed as possible. Also it should be on-premises whenever possible. This will help familiarize the new employee with the location and operation of the food service.

OPERATIONS ORIENTATION

If your new employee will be in a staff support function, he/she will need to understand the operational side of the business and should spend a minimum of two days observing how the business operates. The manager you select should represent a good role model for the company.

During this time the employee should be informed first hand how the projects he/she will be working on will impact the operation of the business. For example, if the new employee is in marketing, assign an operations manager working on the marketing project.

This experience can be a disaster if the manager selected is not capable of communicating a positive image of the company. Like all other facets of your plan, the operations orientation must be planned and not just allowed to happen.

A positive experience can be assured if the orientation plan makes it clear what is to be accomplished. Take time to review the objectives before a new employee is assigned to a project as an observer. Use the Operations Orientation Planning Guide on the next page to make sure you have clearly defined your expectations.

OPERATIONS ORIENTATION PLANNING GUIDE

Day: _____

Time: _____

Manager assigned: _____

Objectives to be accomplished:

_____

_____

_____

Activities to be observed:

_____

_____

_____

_____

Sample questions to discuss:

(1) How does this activity affect my department?

(2) What does my department do well? How could it improve?

(3) What do you do when there is a problem with something my department has done?

(4) What needs to be done to improve the working relationship between my department and your operation?

(5) Was everything accomplished that you planned to achieve?

CLOSING THE DAY

The way the first day ends is just as important as the way it began. On the way home the new employee will reflect on what took place. Closing on a positive note will give the employee a good feeling. The objective is to do everything possible to ensure the new hire looks forward to returning to work the next day.

Before leaving the first day, a manager should spend some private time with the employee. Assuming good effort was put forth on the first day by the employee, communicate directly that you noticed what was accomplished. Review any progress made on any first work assignment. Find something positive to say about it.

End on a positive note, the same way you would when a guest leaves your home. Walk the employee to the door and do your best to make a good parting impression.

Orientation Process

New employee orientation is a process. To this point, considerable emphasis has been placed on the first day activities because they are critical. However, the orientation process will continue over several days or weeks.

An employee cannot learn everything the first day. In your effort to make the new person feel welcome, limit how much information is communicated. It is better to spread important information over several days than to cover everything at once. Having a written plan will help keep you on track.

The Sample Orientation Plan on the facing page will help pull together the pieces that have been discussed. Use it along with the checklists, and the Orientation Template (page 74) and you will deliver a quality program.

SAMPLE ORIENTATION PLAN

WEEK ONE

Orientation to Company Policies and Procedures (Days 1-2)

Day One:

____ Meet with employee (breakfast if possible)

____ Provide Company History

____ Tour Facility, explain parking, building security

____ Introduce to co-workers, show work area

____ Distribute required paperwork

____ Provide and/or explain system for office supplies

____ Provide and discuss job description

____ Distribute Operations Manual (if any)

Review Policies and Procedures:

____ Normal Working Hours

____ Pay Days/Salary

____ Incentive Plan (if any)

____ Performance Review Policies

____ New Hire Probation Period

____ Vacation/Holidays

____ Sick Leave

____ Other Benefits

____ Dress/Appearance Code (if any)

____ Telephone Procedures

____ Employee Discounts

____ Lunch Facilities

____ Review Operations Training Plan/Assignments

____ Make First Job Assigment

It is recommended that the balance of day one and most of day two be spent on the first job assignment.

SAMPLE ORIENTATION PLAN

Operations Orientation (Days 3-4)

_____ Work opening shift
—Employee shadows management and performs assigned tasks
under supervision.

_____ Work closing shift
—Employee shadows management and performs assigned tasks
under supervision.

Review/Job Assignments (Day 5)

_____ Write a short report on operations experience. Include observations,
suggestions, and questions.
_____ Continue work on first job assignment.
_____ Receive additional job assignments.
_____ Review Staff Orientation Schedule.

WEEK TWO

Orientation to Staff Functions (Days 6-10)

—Schedule meeting with staff members to discuss functions, organization and
interface with the new employee.
—Staff members to be selected by the employee's manager.
—Written schedule to be developed and sent to all who will be meeting with the
new employee.
—Employee should have a prepared list of questions to ensure quality of
meeting time.

Supervisor Follow-Up (Days 1-10)

—Supervisor should meet regularly with the new employee during the first
two weeks to answer questions and insure that everything is going according
to plan.

SAMPLE ORIENTATION PLAN

WEEK TWO:

Monday

9:00—9:45	Roland Jackson	Account Manager
11:00—11:45	Janice Wilson	Advertising Coordinator
1:30—2:00	Bob Simpson	Finance Department
3:00—3:45	Russel Miller	Operations Director
4:45—5:00	Meet with Supervisor	

Tuesday

9:00—9:45	Parker Johnson	Research and Development
10:30—11:00	Cheryl Fontaine	Purchasing
12:00—1:00	Lunch with Susan Carson, Personnel Manager	
3:00—3:30	Sam Nordick	Legal Department
4:45—5:00	Meet with Supervisor	

Note: A copy of the orientation schedule would be sent to each person on the list, highlighting the scheduled meeting time.

Meetings can be spread over as many days as necessary. No more than four meetings should be scheduled on one day. This permits the employee to work on the first job assignment and not to be overwhelmed by meeting a lot of new people.

PART IV: ORIENTATION FOR PART-TIME WORKERS

DO YOU NEED A FAST TRACK ORIENTATION PROGRAM?

Answer each question below. If you answer ''yes'' to any question, you should consider developing a Fast Track Orientation for part-time workers as part of your company's overall orientation program.

1. Does your annualized employee turnover exceed 75%?   Yes   No

2. Do you rely on seasonal part-time help (i.e., Christmas, summer)?   Yes   No

3. Does a segment of employees work (by plan) for less than a full year?   Yes   No

4. Does your organization continually hire, orient and train new workers?   Yes   No

5. Would regularly scheduled group orientation meetings save your organization time?   Yes   No

If you answered ''yes'' to any of the above, a Fast Track Orientation should be considered in addition to any standard program. The Fast Track program is especially useful for special circumstances or needs that you experience.

WHO NEEDS A FAST TRACK ORIENTATION?

Many organizations routinely hire, orient and train several employees at the same time. This occurs frequently when:

(1) High turnover is the norm,

(2) Employees are hired for short, specified periods of time, (i.e. holidays).

(3) The organization is large and always has new people coming on board.

Restaurants and fast-food establishments frequently face this situation. Any business that uses student workers will face hiring and training periods at the beginning of the summer and each new school term. Large companies always have staff openings that need to be filled. It is not unusual for some organizations to have a 100% turnover in staff each year.

Retail stores that rely heavily on seasonal business must add many new employees to meet customer demands. These employees have to be oriented and trained in a short period of time.

In situations like the above, a supervisor's time is limited. With many new employees starting at one time, a fast track program can orient several employees in a short period of time.

SPECIAL PROBLEMS AND OPPORTUNITIES

Orientation for employees who may be on board for only a few weeks is just as important as for those who are starting a career. In fact, probably more important because these employees must become productive immediately. Until they have been oriented and provided with some basic training, new employees won't be very productive.

The orientation process for fast track programs must be squeezed into a short period of time. It is imperative, therefore, to have an organized program.

A regular orientation schedule makes it possible for a new employee to be oriented within a few days after starting. Because time is so critical some companies have a one day orientation on the first day followed immediately by skills training. The employee may later attend a more formal orientation meeting scheduled for all new employees.

FAST TRACK OBJECTIVES

The objectives for a Fast Track Orientation are the same as for a standard orientation:

☐ Provide a welcome;

☐ Develop positive perceptions;

☐ Confirm job decision;

☐ Speed training to make the new employee productive as quickly as possible;

☐ Put the employee at ease.

The irony is that you should have the same quality orientation for an employee who may be with you for six weeks, as for one that will be with you for six years. The only difference is that it must be done more quickly.

Large companies that add new employees on a regular basis will benefit from the "Fast Track" concept. A generic program can be used over and over to cover general information that all employees need to know. Specific items can then be covered by the new employee's supervisor during other periods in the orientation process.

This approach builds in flexibility for both the supervisor and the employee and can make the difference between success and failure with a fast track program. A program must take into consideration the supervisor's need for having a productive employee in a short period of time. The supervisor needs a program that covers the basics quickly and still allows a focus on skills training. In a fast track environment, a portion of the responsibility for orientation is often shifted from the supervisor to others in the organization.

HOW TO DO IT AND WHAT TO COVER

There are several things you can do to have an effective Fast Track Orientation:

—Use a mini-orientation package.

—Prepare a ''canned'' overview covering basic information about the organization/job.

—Conduct group meetings.

—Share orientation responsibilities with other supervisors.

—Prepare orientation handout packets.

Each of these items is described in this section as part of a total orientation program. They may be modified as necessary to meet your organization's needs.

Let's take a closer look at each item.

Mini Orientation Package

A mini orientation package will save considerable time for a supervisor who has several new employees starting together. This package contains the minimum paperwork a new employee needs to complete. Included are:

—Form W-4 for withholding.

—Form I-9, Employment Eligibility Verification.

—Employee Agreement.

—Payroll Form.

—Critical policies (i.e. alcohol, cash handling, etc.).

—Probation Form (if applicable).

—Employee Handbook (if available).

MINI-ORIENTATION PACKAGE

The objective is for a supervisor to orient the new employee quickly so training can begin. All of the items on the Orientation Checklist shown on page 72 need to be covered, but many can wait until later after the employee has been on the job a few days. For example, company history may be important, but will not be necessary before the employee begins his/her training.

All of the necessary paperwork should be placed in a packet that can be handed to the new employee. This preparation will save time since a supervisor won't have to chase down the forms and put together a packet every time a new employee starts. As each item is completed it should be put back in the folder and returned to the supervisor.

When the new employee attends the group meeting, the rest of the orientation information can be presented.

The checklist on the facing page will help you put together a mini-orientation package.

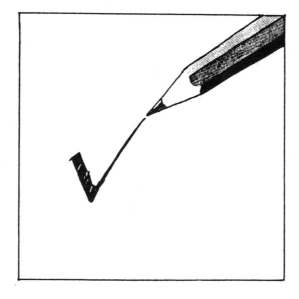

MINI-ORIENTATION PACKAGE
(Continued)

The purpose of the mini-orientation package is to give a new employee the minimum information necessary to:

1. Satisfy government and company regulations, and

2. Answer questions that, if unanswered, could slow the employee's productivity.

Some sample items are listed below.

____ Application Form	____ Pay Days
____ W-4 Form	____ Probation Form
____ I-9 Form	____ Employee Handbook
____ Employee Agreement	____ Dress/Uniform Code
____ Payroll Form	____ Critical Policies
____ Benefit Enrollment	

*Add your Own:

____ _____   ____ _____

____ _____   ____ _____

---

*Before you put anything in the package, ask ''Could the employee start training without having to worry about this item?'' If your answer is ''Yes''—the item should *not* be included in the Mini-Orientation Package. It can wait until later. If you answer, ''No'', it should be included.

PREPARE A PACKAGED OVERVIEW

A packaged overview can be developed to orient new employees to the organization and the job. The presentation can be used over and over, whenever needed.

One approach is to produce an audio-visual presentation that presents a consistent message to all new employees. The format can be cassette/workbook, slide/tape or video tape.

When a new employee is hired, a supervisor arranges to have the program presented. This saves supervisor time and helps present a professional image of the company to the new employee.

Properly done, a quality packaged program will allow the company to sell itself to the new employee and help affirm the employee's decision to join your organization. This type of program should not be "thrown together." A well developed program should be both motivating and informative. If your organization doesn't have the talent and resources to produce it inside, you may want to consider getting outside help.

Once you have a program, you will find other uses for it, such as a recruiting tool or as a motivational reminder to current employees.

Some topics that lend themselves to a packaged presentation include:

—Mission and Philosophy,

—Company history,

—Organization structure,

—Company position in the marketplace,

—Commitment to service,

—etc.

The presentation can be enhanced with some brief upbeat remarks by the company president or other key executives.

Appropriate music and visual images can project a quality image of the organization. A packaged program should last approximately 15–20 minutes. If it is longer it can start to sound self-serving.

Use the checklist on the next page as a guide to develop a packaged program.

PACKAGED ORIENTATION PROGRAM PLANNING

Make notes on the outline below of specific items your organization wants to present in a packaged program.

  I. Mission Statement

     A. Introduction by President and CEO

     B. Business philosophy

  II. Our Organization

     A. Who we are

     B. What we do

  III. Major Products and Commitment to the Customer

  IV. Company History

  V. What You Can Expect as an Employee of this Organization

     A. Employee success stories

     B. Employee testimonials

  VI. Future Outlook

     A. New Products

     B. New Locations

     C. New Jobs

CONDUCT GROUP MEETINGS

Group meetings should cover basic information. This will save considerable time. For example, one two-hour meeting with 10 employees rather than 10 two-hour individual meetings, will save 18 hours.

A successful meeting requires planning. The person conducting it must be comfortable in front of a group. This section will provide guidelines for planning the meeting. If you need help getting up in front of groups, read Steve Mandel's book, **Effective Presentation Skills.**

A successful meeting starts with an **agenda** geared to meet your objectives. This agenda should list key activities that will be covered during the meeting and be designed to:

(1) Keep you on track;

(2) Let the meeting participants know what to expect.

It should include the names and titles of those who will be making presentations. This will help new employees associate names, faces and job titles.

In most cases, the preliminary meeting should not last more than two hours. During this time most basics should be covered.

If you use the Mini Orientation Package described earlier, the meeting can answer questions about items an employee has already experienced on the job. It also allows extra time for other items you feel are critical.

The Checklist on page 72 can help set an agenda which will answer the questions—who, what, when, and where. Refer to the sample agenda for details. Several items covered in the meeting can be reinforced with orientation handout packets. The development of these packets will be discussed later in this section.

SAMPLE ORIENTATION MEETING AGENDA

Tuesday, March 1 — Main Conference Room

8:00 - 8:20	Welcome/Introductions/Purpose	**Bob Smith** Operations Manager
8:20 - 8:40	Company History	**Bob Smith**
8:40 - 9:00	Company Operations	**Cindy Parks** Operations Vice President
9:00 - 9:20	Employee Benefits	**Dan Sellers** Benefits
9:20 - 9:30	Break	
9:30 - 10:00	Paperwork/Questions and Answers	**Bob Smith**
10:00	Adjourn for tour of the work place	

ARRANGE A MEETING PLACE

Once you have an agenda, the next step is to arrange the **meeting place.** If practical, hold it in a nicely appointed conference area (such as a board room). This will give the message that you consider the new employees to be ''special'' and have taken extra steps to meet their needs.

The set-up of the meeting room can also contribute to the success of the orientation. The best is one in which all attendees can see each other. This creates a sense of togetherness and encourages people to get to know each other.

If possible, you might consider a horseshoe or U-shape arrangement. The presenter can easily see all participants and make frequent eye contact. This set up also makes distribution of materials easier. A typical set up would look like this:

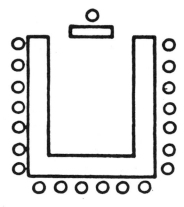

ARRANGE A MEETING PLACE
(Continued)

If you are not able to use the U-shape, consider the hollow square or conference style. This simply fills the opening and allows for a few more seats.

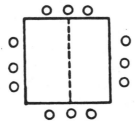

If this won't work, use the traditional classroom format. The major drawback here is that people will be looking over the backs of heads. It is difficult for the participants to see the others without turning around or straining. Sometimes, however, when the group is large, this is the only choice.

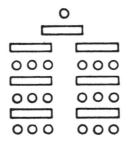

It is important to have tables available, or chairs with arms that allow writing. This gives participants room to place materials, take notes, or fill out paperwork.

Once the agenda is set and the meeting place is determined, the details should be communicated to those who will be attending.

Whenever possible a written notice is best. This insures a consistent message (time, date, location, etc.) is received by all who attend. It does not, however, ensure everyone will read it. Some companies have found that a telephone confirmation follow-up will help insure participants know the specifics about the meeting and plan to attend.

SHARE RESPONSIBILITY FOR THE PRESENTATION

When planning the meeting, assignments should be provided to others who will be involved. This is important when you have employees who will be working with different managers or supervisors.

Be sure to prepare each presenter for what you want him/her to accomplish in the meeting. A rehearsal of the presentation is recommended. This way you will know what each person plans to say and how long the presentation will take. Rehearsal allows you to eliminate duplication or add material that might otherwise not be covered. Getting everyone involved will make the meeting more interesting and reduce your work load.

Have a Written Plan

Start by making a list of items on the agenda to be presented. Assign presenters a topic about which they are knowledgeable. This is best when you have a short time to prepare for the meeting and the presenters are the subject matter experts. For example, a representative from personnel should discuss the benefits program whenever possible.

Remember, a major objective of orientation is to develop positive perceptions. One disorganized presentation can offset the other good things you do during the meeting. Don't skimp on the preparation—it will be evident to all who attend if you are well organized.

PREPARE ORIENTATION PACKETS

Much of what you need for one new employee will be repeated for every new hire. Use the Orientation Checklists and Template provided to determine what materials would be effective handouts at your orientation meetings.

Develop a packet that can be given to each person at an appropriate time during the meeting. You may want to duplicate some items that are included in the Mini Orientation Package. Use the meeting to review the contents of the packet with the participants.

The packet should be as easy to handle as possible. A recommended approach is to use a **file folder packet.** Prepare a file folder for each person to be oriented. Insert all of the information in the sequence you want it to be read.

During the meeting it might be appropriate for employees to complete required paperwork. Once completed, the paperwork can be placed back in the file folder. Rather than spending time during the meeting collecting papers, or afterwards collating forms into individual folders, you can have a completed file folder for each employee. Having employees complete forms at the same time encourages them to fill in the information accurately and completely. They can ask questions that may benefit the group if something is unclear.

ORIENTATION HANDBOOK

A variation on the file folder packet is to insert an orientation handbook inside the file folder. This handbook should contain all the forms the new employee needs to complete. Place these in a three ring binder so they can be easily removed. Setting up a handbook in this manner will save time.

At the appropriate time during the meeting, you can distribute the file folder and orientation handbook. When the forms are completed, they can be removed from the handbook and placed in individual file folders.

Regardless of which method you use, the goal is to make the orientation process go smoothly and take care of the administrative details for new employees.

By developing each component described in this section:

—Mini Orientation Package,

—Packaged Overview Program,

—Group Meetings,

—Shared Orientation Responsibilities, and

—Orientation Handout Packets,

you will have a well organized and professional Fast Track Orientation program.

CASE STUDY

FAST TRACK OR OFF TRACK?

Joe Sherman, a senior at Woodware High School, decided to enter the world of work. He was hired as a cook at Bob's Better Burgers and told to report on Monday, two hours before the restaurant opened.

When Joe arrived he was greeted by Bob, who handed him a packet of forms. Joe was asked to fill out the forms and put them back in the packet. Joe was directed to a seat in the dining room where two other new employees were already filling out forms.

Joe had a question about one form so he asked one of the new hires about it, since Bob was out of the room. Together the new employees decided the best way to fill in the form. A few minutes later two more new employees arrived and were told to start on their packets. As they sat down, Bob took the first two employees into a corner and to show them a video tape about the parent company. Joe worked on the rest of his paperwork, while ignoring the noise from the video.

When the video ended, the first two employees were taken to the kitchen. Joe was then told to watch the video. Next, Joe was taken to the kitchen and trained on operating the French Fry machine. The two new employees who were ahead of him had finished their French Fry training and were learning about the grill.

Evaluate Bob's orientation techniques.

What things were good? _____

_____

What things could be improved? _____

_____

What do you think Joe Sherman's impression was of his first day on the job? _____

_____

SUMMARY

A Fast Track Orientation process allows several new employees to start together and learn about their new organization in a consistent manner.

Fast Track Orientation is not a substitute for a thorough process that takes place over several days or weeks. It can be used to get the ball rolling and should be considered as the first phase of a more complete orientation process for permanent employees.

During Fast Track Orientation essential information is covered and the stage is set for the things such as operations orientation. Giving the first job assignment and reviewing the job description are other examples of tasks that may not lend themselves to the Fast Track Orientation process.

Fast Track Orientation can help get a new employee productive quickly when used in conjunction with the rest of your orientation plan. This will save a supervisor time, benefit the employee, the organization and ultimately the customer.

PART IV: SELF ASSESSMENT

The following items summarize the key points covered in Part IV. Check the appropriate space.

	Have Available	Should Modify	Need To Develop
Mini Orientation Package	_____	_____	_____
Packaged Overview	_____	_____	_____
Group Meetings	_____	_____	_____
—Agenda	_____	_____	_____
—Meeting Place	_____	_____	_____
—Assigned Presenters	_____	_____	_____
—Written Plan	_____	_____	_____
Orientation Handout Packets	_____	_____	_____

Other items:

_____ _____ _____ _____

_____ _____ _____ _____

_____ _____ _____ _____

Review this list prior to your next major need for hiring, orientation and training. For example, if you bring on Christmas help November 15, review your Fast Track Orientation in September. That will give you time to update existing materials and start development of others you need.

PART V: PUTTING IT ALL TOGETHER

PUTTING IT ALL TOGETHER

Effective new employee orientation requires planning, execution, and follow up. By following the steps in this book, you should have completed an evaluation of your existing program and identified areas for improvement.

As a final check, review the Orientation Checklists on the next two pages to make sure you have identified all of the pieces you need to develop.

Use the Orientation Template to develop your own specific new employee orientation **PLAN**.

Once developed you will be ready to put it into practice (**EXECUTE**).

Then you need to **FOLLOW UP** regularly to see that it is working as you intended.

This cycle of plan, execute, and follow up, should continue until the program meets the objectives you set on page 1.

ORIENTATION CHECKLIST

The items listed below are the most common that should be covered during new employee orientation.

The items are listed in three categories. You may wish to define your own categories. The important thing is to have a comprehensive list and to cover all the items.

Administrative

_____ Employment Application

_____ Employee Benefits

_____ W-4 Form

_____ Non-Compete Agreement

_____ Insurance Forms

_____ _____

Personal

_____ Work Area

_____ Building Tour

_____ Introduction to Co-workers

_____ Parking

_____ Time Off

_____ Vacations/Holidays

_____ Dress/Appearance/Uniforms

_____ Mail

_____ Probation Period

_____ Sick Pay

_____ Telephone Procedures

_____ Employee Discounts

_____ Personal Use of Equipment

_____ _____

Business

_____ Job Description

_____ Organization Chart

_____ Hours/Work Schedule

_____ Pay Rate/Pay Days

_____ Incentive Plan

_____ Operations Manuals

_____ Operations Orientation

_____ Company Policies

_____ Confidentiality

_____ Company History

_____ Office Supplies

_____ Company Publications

_____ Employee Handbook

_____ I.D. Card

_____ _____

Miscellaneous

_____ Recreation Activities

_____ Local Items of Interest

_____ _____

ORIENTATION CHECKLIST
(Continued)

Have you prepared for the new employee's arrival by:

_____ Preparing a written orientation plan?

_____ Designating a work area (office, desk, etc.)?

_____ Assigning a phone number?

_____ Arranging for office supplies?

_____ Preparing required paperwork and forms for completion?

_____ Keeping your schedule free to meet with the new employee?

_____ Arranging for lunch the first day?

_____ Scheduling staff orientation meetings?

_____ Scheduling an operations orientation?

_____ Providing a welcoming get together?

_____ Preparing first job assignment?

_____ Making available copies of appropriate company manuals and publications?

What specifically will you do to:

Provide A Welcome   **Develop Positive Perceptions**

_____   _____

_____   _____

Confirm Job Decision   **Speed Training**

_____   _____

_____   _____

Put Employee at Ease   **Other**

_____   _____

_____   _____

ORIENTATION TEMPLATE

Use this template to create your own individual orientation plan.

_____   _____
Employee   Job Title

_____   _____
Supervisor   Start Date

I. Preparation

____ Publicity about employee   ____ Designated work area

____ Office supplies   ____ Paperwork and forms

____ Quiet place to meet   ____ Welcoming get together

____ Arrangements for lunch

II. Activities

Administrative   **Personal**

____ _____   ____ _____

____ _____   ____ _____

____ _____   ____ _____

____ _____   ____ _____

____ _____   ____ _____

____ _____   ____ _____

____ _____   ____ _____

____ _____   ____ _____

ORIENTATION TEMPLATE

Business   **Miscellaneous**

____ _____   ____ _____

____ _____   ____ _____

____ _____   ____ _____

____ _____   ____ _____

____ _____   ____ _____

____ _____   ____ _____

____ _____   ____ _____

III: Operations Orientation

Day/Date   Hours   **Manager**

_____   _____   _____

Activities to be accomplished:

_____

_____

_____

Day/Date   Hours   **Manager**

_____   _____   _____

Activities to be accomplished:

_____

_____

_____

ORIENTATION TEMPLATE

IV. Staff Orientation

Day/Date: _____

Time	Person	Title/Department
_____	_____	_____
_____	_____	_____
_____	_____	_____
_____	_____	_____

Day/Date: _____

Time	Person	Title/Department
_____	_____	_____
_____	_____	_____
_____	_____	_____
_____	_____	_____

Day/Date: _____

Time	Person	Title/Department
_____	_____	_____
_____	_____	_____
_____	_____	_____

Day/Date: _____

Time	Person	Title/Department
_____	_____	_____
_____	_____	_____
_____	_____	_____

ORDER FORM
THE FIFTY-MINUTE SERIES

Quantity	Title	Code #	Price	Amount
	MANAGEMENT TRAINING			
	Self-Managing Teams	00-0	$7.95	
	Delegating for Results	008-6	$7.95	
	Successful Negotiation — Revised	09-2	$7.95	
	Increasing Employee Productivity	10-8	$7.95	
	Personal Performance Contracts — Revised	12-2	$7.95	
	Team Building — Revised	16-5	$7.95	
	Effective Meeting Skills	33-5	$7.95	
	An Honest Day's Work: Motivating Employees	39-4	$7.95	
	Managing Disagreement Constructively	41-6	$7.95	
	Learning To Lead	43-4	$7.95	
	The Fifty-Minute Supervisor — 2/e	58-0	$7.95	
	Leadership Skills for Women	62-9	$7.95	
	Coaching & Counseling	68-8	$7.95	
	Ethics in Business	69-6	$7.95	
	Understanding Organizational Change	71-8	$7.95	
	Project Management	75-0	$7.95	
	Risk Taking	076-9	$7.95	
	Managing Organizational Change	80-7	$7.95	
	Working Together in a Multi-Cultural Organization	85-8	$7.95	
	Selecting And Working With Consultants	87-4	$7.95	
	Empowerment	096-5	$7.95	
	Managing for Commitment	099-X	$7.95	
	Rate Your Skills as a Manager	101-5	$7.95	
	PERSONNEL/HUMAN RESOURCES			
	Your First Thirty Days: A Professional Image in a New Job	003-5	$7.95	
	Office Management: A Guide to Productivity	005-1	$7.95	
	Men and Women: Partners at Work	009-4	$7.95	
	Effective Performance Appraisals — Revised	11-4	$7.95	
	Quality Interviewing — Revised	13-0	$7.95	
	Personal Counseling	14-9	$7.95	
	Giving and Receiving Criticism	023-X	$7.95	
	Attacking Absenteeism	042-6	$7.95	
	New Employee Orientation	46-7	$7.95	
	Professional Excellence for Secretaries	52-1	$7.95	
	Guide to Affirmative Action	54-8	$7.95	
	Writing a Human Resources Manual	70-X	$7.95	
	Downsizing Without Disaster	081-7	$7.95	
	Winning at Human Relations	86-6	$7.95	
	High Performance Hiring	088-4	$7.95	
	COMMUNICATIONS			
	Technical Writing in the Corporate World	004-3	$7.95	
	Effective Presentation Skills	24-6	$7.95	
	Better Business Writing — Revised	25-4	$7.95	

Quantity	Title	Code #	Price	Amount
COMMUNICATIONS (continued)				
	The Business of Listening	34-3	$7.95	
	Writing Fitness	35-1	$7.95	
	The Art of Communicating	45-9	$7.95	
	Technical Presentation Skills	55-6	$7.95	
	Making Humor Work	61-0	$7.95	
	50 One Minute Tips to Better Communication	071-X	$7.95	
	Speed-Reading in Business	78-5	$7.95	
	Influencing Others	84-X	$7.95	
PERSONAL IMPROVEMENT				
	Attitude: Your Most Priceless Possession — Revised	011-6	$7.95	
	Personal Time Management	22-X	$7.95	
	Successful Self-Management	26-2	$7.95	
	Business Etiquette And Professionalism	32-9	$7.95	
	Balancing Home & Career — Revised	35-3	$7.95	
	Developing Positive Assertiveness	38-6	$7.95	
	The Telephone and Time Management	53-X	$7.95	
	Memory Skills in Business	56-4	$7.95	
	Developing Self-Esteem	66-1	$7.95	
	Managing Personal Change	74-2	$7.95	
	Finding Your Purpose	072-8	$7.95	
	Concentration!	073-6	$7.95	
	Plan Your Work/Work Your Plan!	078-7	$7.95	
	Stop Procrastinating: Get To Work!	88-2	$7.95	
	12 Steps to Self-Improvement	102-3	$7.95	
CREATIVITY				
	Systematic Problem Solving & Decision Making	63-7	$7.95	
	Creativity in Business	67-X	$7.95	
	Intuitive Decision Making	098-1	$7.95	
TRAINING				
	Training Managers to Train	43-2	$7.95	
	Visual Aids in Business	77-7	$7.95	
	Developing Instructional Design	076-0	$7.95	
	Training Methods That Work	082-5	$7.95	
WELLNESS				
	Mental Fitness: A Guide to Emotional Health	15-7	$7.95	
	Wellness in the Workplace	020-5	$7.95	
	Personal Wellness	21-3	$7.95	
	Preventing Job Burnout	23-8	$7.95	
	Job Performance and Chemical Dependency	27-0	$7.95	
	Overcoming Anxiety	29-9	$7.95	
	Productivity at the Workstation	41-8	$7.95	
	Healthy Strategies for Working Women	079-5	$7.95	
CUSTOMER SERVICE/SALES TRAINING				
	Sales Training Basics — Revised	02-5	$7.95	
	Restaurant Server's Guide — Revised	08-4	$7.95	
	Effective Sales Management	31-0	$7.95	

Quantity	Title	Code #	Price	Amount
	CUSTOMER SERVICE/SALES TRAINING (continued)			
	Professional Selling	42-4	$7.95	
	Telemarketing Basics	60-2	$7.95	
	Telephone Courtesy & Customer Service — Revised	64-7	$7.95	
	Calming Upset Customers	65-3	$7.95	
	Quality at Work	72-6	$7.95	
	Managing Quality Customer Service	83-1	$7.95	
	Customer Satisfaction — Revised	84-1	$7.95	
	Quality Customer Service — Revised	95-5	$7.95	
	SMALL BUSINESS/FINANCIAL PLANNING			
	Consulting for Success	006-X	$7.95	
	Understanding Financial Statements	22-1	$7.95	
	Marketing Your Consulting or Professional Services	40-8	$7.95	
	Starting Your New Business	44-0	$7.95	
	Direct Mail Magic	075-2	$7.95	
	Credits & Collections	080-9	$7.95	
	Publicity Power	82-3	$7.95	
	Writing & Implementing Your Marketing Plan	083-3	$7.95	
	Personal Financial Fitness — Revised	89-0	$7.95	
	Financial Planning With Employee Benefits	90-4	$7.95	
	ADULT LITERACY/BASIC LEARNING			
	Returning to Learning: Getting Your G.E.D.	02-7	$7.95	
	Study Skills Strategies — Revised	05-X	$7.95	
	The College Experience	07-8	$7.95	
	Basic Business Math	24-8	$7.95	
	Becoming an Effective Tutor	28-0	$7.95	
	Reading Improvement	086-8	$7.95	
	Introduction to Microcomputers	087-6	$7.95	
	Clear Writing	094-9	$7.95	
	Building Blocks of Business Writing	095-7	$7.95	
	Language, Customs & Protocol	097-3	$7.95	
	CAREER BUILDING			
	Career Discovery	07-6	$7.95	
	Effective Networking	30-2	$7.95	
	Preparing for Your Interview	33-7	$7.95	
	Plan B: Protecting Your Career	48-3	$7.95	
	I Got The Job!	59-9	$7.95	
	Job Search That Works	105-8	$7.95	

NOTE: ORDERS TOTALING LESS THAN $25.00 MUST BE PREPAID

	Amount
Total Books	
Less Discount	
Total	
California Tax (California residents add 7%)	
Shipping	
TOTAL	

☐ Please send me a free Video Catalog.   ☐ Please add my name to your mailing list.

☐ Mastercard   ☐ VISA   ☐ AMEX   Exp. Date _____

Account No. _____   Name (as appears on card) _____

Ship to: _____   Bill to: _____

_____   _____

_____   _____

_____   _____

Phone number: _____   P.O. #: _____

All orders of less than $25.00 must be prepaid. Bill to orders require a company P.O.#. For more information, call (415) 949-4888 or FAX (415) 949-1610.

BUSINESS REPLY MAIL
FIRST CLASS   PERMIT NO. 884   LOS ALTOS, CA

POSTAGE WILL BE PAID BY ADDRESSEE

Crisp Publications, Inc.
95 First Street
Los Altos, CA 94022